CHEERS FOR CAREERS!

I WANT TO BE A WELDER

by Julie Murray

Cody Koala
An Imprint of Pop!
popbooksonline.com

Hello! My name is Cody Koala

This book is filled with videos, puzzles, games, and more! Scan the QR codes* while you read, or visit the website below to make this book pop.

popbooksonline.com/welder

*Scanning QR codes requires a web-enabled smart device with a QR code reader app and a camera.

abdobooks.com

Published by Pop!, a division of ABDO, PO Box 398166, Minneapolis, Minnesota 55439.

Printed in the United States of America North Mankato, Minnesota.

052024
082024

THIS BOOK CONTAINS RECYCLED MATERIALS

Cover Photo: Shutterstock Images
Interior Photos: Shutterstock Images
Editor: Elizabeth Andrews and Grace Hansen
Series Designer: Colleen McLaren

Library of Congress Control Number: 2023947429

Publisher's Cataloging-in-Publication Data

Names: Murray, Julie, author.
Title: I want to be a welder / by Julie Murray
Description: Minneapolis, Minnesota : Pop!, 2025 | Series: Cheers for careers! | Includes online resources and index
Identifiers: ISBN 9781098246075 (lib. bdg.) | ISBN 9781098246631 (ebook)
Subjects: LCSH: Welders (Persons)--Juvenile literature. | Welding--Juvenile literature. | Metal-work--Juvenile literature. | Servicing trades--Juvenile literature. | Occupations--Juvenile literature.
Classification: DDC 671.5--dc23

Table of Contents

Chapter 1

Joining Materials

Welders use heat and tools to join or repair metal. They apply heat to the metal objects they are working with to bond them together.

More than 50% of all man-made products require welding.

Watch a video here!

Welding can be a dangerous job. Safety gear is needed! A welding helmet and goggles protect the head and face. A jacket, gloves, and pants protect the rest of the body. Heavy shoes are needed too.

The sparks that fly from a welder's blowtorch are small pieces of melted metal.

Chapter 2

Skills Needed

Welders need to have good math skills. They measure objects and do **calculations**. They should also be able to read detailed plans called welding blueprints.

Learn more here!

welding magnet

chipping hammer

angle grinder

clamp

welding machine

welding helmet and gloves

Welders need steady hands. They use many different tools. They work with **torches**, angle grinders, and magnets.

Burns are the most common injuries in welding.

Attention to detail is a skill all welders need. Welders must also be able to focus

for long periods of time. Being careless can result in dangerous injuries.

Chapter 3

How to Become a Welder

A community college or welding program is a good place to start training to become a welder. Some jobs require a **certification**.

Welders are in high demand in the United States.

Explore links here!

An **apprenticeship** is a great way to get welding experience. This hands-on work will provide a solid base for the career.

Chapter 4

Different Jobs

There are many types of jobs in welding. Welders can work in **manufacturing** and **construction**. Working with cars, ships, and aircraft are options too.

Complete an activity here!

Welders use their hands all day. Melting objects together with intense heat requires specific skills and great focus. Welding is a rewarding career!

Some welders work underwater!

Making Connections

Text-to-Self

If you were a welder where would you like to work? Why?

Text-to-Text

Can you think of a book that discusses a building or object that might have needed welding? If so, did you learn anything different in that book?

Text-to-World

Welders work with their hands. What other careers require people to work with their hands?

Glossary

apprenticeship – an arrangement in which someone learns a trade under an expert.

calculation – the process of getting an answer to a number question by adding, subtracting, multiplying, or dividing.

certification – proof of having fulfilled certain training requirements.

construction – the building of something, typically a large structure.

manufacturing – the process of making things by hand or by machinery.

torch – a long metal stem usually bent at an angle that applies direct, intense heat to a material.

Index

Online Resources

popbooksonline.com

Thanks for reading this Cody Koala book!

This book is filled with videos, puzzles, games, and more! Scan the QR codes* while you read, or visit the website below to make this book pop.

popbooksonline.com/welder

*Scanning QR codes requires a web-enabled smart device with a QR code reader app and a camera.